St Paul

Prayer Book

FAMILY PUBLICATIONS

ISBN 9781871217834

published by
Family Publications
Denis Riches House, 66 Sandford Lane,
Kennington, Oxford OX1 5RP
www.familypublications.co.uk

Printed in England through
s|s|media ltd

S aint Paul speaks . . . of a kind of prayer which arises from the depths of our hearts in sighs too deep for words, in 'groanings' (Rom 8:26) inspired by the Spirit. This is a prayer which yearns, in the midst of chastisement, for the fulfilment of God's promises. It is a prayer of unfailing hope, but also one of patient endurance and, often, accompanied by suffering for the truth. Through this prayer, we share in the mystery of Christ's own weakness and suffering, while trusting firmly in the victory of his Cross.

Pope Benedict XVI
17 April 2008

Prayer to Saint Paul the Apostle

Holy Apostle who, with your teachings and with your charity, have taught the entire world, look kindly upon us, your children and disciples. We expect everything from your prayers to the Divine Master and to Mary, Queen of the Apostles. Grant, Doctor of the Gentiles, that we may live by faith, be saved by hope, and that charity alone reign in us. Obtain for us, vessel of election, docile correspondence to divine grace, so that it may not remain unfruitful in us. Grant that we may ever better know you, love you, and imitate you; that we may be living members of the Church, the Mystical Body of Jesus Christ. Raise up many and holy apostles. May the warm breath of true charity permeate the entire world. Grant that all may know and glorify God and the Divine Master, Way and Truth and Life.

And, Lord Jesus, you know we have no faith in our own powers. In your mercy grant that we may be defended against all adversity, through the powerful intercession of St Paul our teacher.

Amen

Tarsus stands on the southern coast of modern Turkey. When Saul was born here, it was the capital of the Roman province of Cilicia.

❝ *Paul replied, 'I am a Jew, from Tarsus in Cilicia, a citizen of no mean city.'* ❞

Acts 21: 39

A Citizen of No Mean City

'I am a Jew, born at Tarsus in Cilicia, but brought up in this city at the feet of Gamaliel, educated according to the strict manner of the law of our fathers, being zealous for God as you all are this day. I persecuted this Way to the death, binding and delivering to prison both men and women, as the high priest and the whole council of elders bear me witness. From them I received letters to the brethren, and I journeyed to Damascus to take those also who were there and bring them in bonds to Jerusalem to be punished.'

Acts 22: 3-5

O Glorious Saint Paul, after persecuting the Church you became by God's grace her most zealous Apostle. Help us to be inspired by your Epistles and to partake of your indomitable love for Jesus, so that we may join you in praising him in heaven for all eternity.

Amen

The Prayer of Saint Paul

Blessed be the God and Father of our Lord Jesus Christ, who has blessed us in Christ with every spiritual blessing in the heavenly places, even as he chose us in him before the foundation of the world, that we should be holy and blameless before him. He destined us in love to be his sons through Jesus Christ, according to the purpose of his will, to the praise of his glorious grace which he freely bestowed on us in the Beloved. In him we have redemption through his blood, the forgiveness of our trespasses, according to the riches of his grace which he lavished upon us. For he has made known to us in all wisdom and insight the mystery of his will, according to his purpose which he set forth in Christ as a plan for the fullness of time, to unite all things in him, things in heaven and things on earth.

Ephesians 1: 3-10

The Road to Damascus

'Thus I journeyed to Damascus with the authority and commission of the chief priests. At midday, O king, I saw on the way a light from heaven, brighter than the sun, shining round me and those who journeyed with me. And when we had all fallen to the ground, I heard a voice saying to me in the Hebrew language, "Saul, Saul, why do you persecute me? It hurts you to kick against the goads." And I said, "Who are you, Lord?" And the Lord said, "I am Jesus whom you are persecuting. But rise and stand upon your feet; for I have appeared to you for this purpose, to appoint you to serve and bear witness to the things in which you have seen me and to those in which I will appear to you, delivering you from the people and from the Gentiles – to whom I send you to open their eyes, that they may turn from darkness to light and from the power of Satan to God, that they may receive forgiveness of sins and a place among those who are sanctified by faith in me."'

Acts 26: 12-18

God our Father, you taught the Gospel to all the world through the preaching of Paul your apostle. May we who celebrate his conversion to the faith follow him in bearing witness to the truth.

Amen

Taught by the Spirit

God has revealed to us through the Spirit. For the Spirit searches everything, even the depths of God. For what person knows a man's thoughts except the spirit of the man which is in him? So also no one comprehends the thoughts of God except the Spirit of God. Now we have received not the spirit of the world, but the Spirit which is from God, that we might understand the gifts bestowed on us by God. And we impart this in words not taught by human wisdom but taught by the Spirit, interpreting spiritual truths to those who possess the Spirit.

1 Corinthians 2: 10-13

———•·•———

Lord, the world can offer us nothing except through you. As your Apostle Paul taught the Church, only through your grace can we know God, and only through your Spirit can your grace become fruitful in us. We pray that in all things you may guide us by the light of your Spirit.

Amen

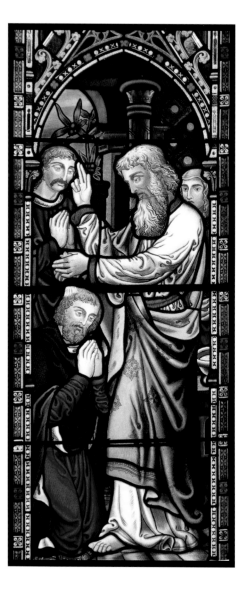

The Image of the Invisible God

He has delivered us from the dominion of darkness and transferred us to the kingdom of his beloved Son, in whom we have redemption, the forgiveness of sins. He is the image of the invisible God, the first-born of all creation; for in him all things were created, in heaven and on earth, visible and invisible, whether thrones or dominions or principalities or authorities – all things were created through him and for him. He is before all things, and in him all things hold together. He is the head of the body, the Church; he is the beginning, the first-born from the dead, that in everything he might be pre-eminent. For in him all the fullness of God was pleased to dwell, and through him to reconcile to himself all things, whether on earth or in heaven, making peace by the blood of his cross.

Colossians 1: 13-20

God, in yourself you are beyond all our understanding, but through your Son you have revealed yourself to us. In Christ were all things made, and through him they have their existence. Grant that, at the end, we may find fulfilment also in Him.

Amen

Almighty and everlasting God, who instructed your blessed Apostle Paul what he should do that he might be filled with the Holy Ghost; grant that we may serve you in fear and trembling, and so be filled with the comfort of your heavenly gifts.

Amen

Obedient unto Death

Do nothing from selfishness or conceit, but in
humility count others better than yourselves.
Let each of you look not only to his own interests, but
also to the interests of others. Have this mind among
yourselves, which is yours in Christ Jesus, who,

Though he was in the form of God,
did not count equality with God a thing to be
grasped,
but emptied himself,
taking the form of a servant, being born in the
likeness of men.
And being found in human form
he humbled himself and became obedient unto
death,
even death on a cross.
Therefore God has highly exalted him
and bestowed on him the name which is above every
name,
that at the name of Jesus every knee should bow,
in heaven and on earth and under the earth,
and every tongue confess that Jesus Christ is Lord,
to the glory of God the Father.

Therefore, my beloved, as you have always obeyed, so
now, not only as in my presence but much more in my
absence, work out your own salvation with fear and
trembling; for God is at work in you, both to will and
to work for his good pleasure.

Philippians 2: 3-13

Litany of Saint Paul the Apostle

Lord have mercy. *Lord have mercy.*
Christ, have mercy. *Christ have mercy.*
Lord have mercy. *Lord have mercy.*

Holy Mary, Mother of God, *Pray for us.*
Queen conceived without original sin, *Pray for us.*

Saint Paul, *Pray for us.*
Apostle of the Gentiles, *Pray for us.*

Vessel of Election, *Pray for us.*
St Paul, who was taken to the third heaven, *Pray for us.*
St Paul, who heard things not given to man to utter, *Pray for us.*
St Paul, who knew nothing but Christ, and Him crucified,
   Pray for us.
St Paul, whose love for Christ was stronger than death, *Pray for us.*
St Paul, who wished to be dissolved and be with Christ, *Pray for us.*
St Paul, whose zeal knew no bounds, *Pray for us.*
St Paul, who made yourself all to all, to gain all to Christ, *Pray for us.*
St Paul, who called yourself prisoner of Christ for us, *Pray for us.*
St Paul, who was jealous of us, with the jealousy of God, *Pray for us.*
St Paul, who glories only in the Cross of Christ, *Pray for us.*
St Paul, who bore in your body the mortification of Christ,
   Pray for us.
St Paul, who exclaimed: With Christ I am nailed to the cross!
   Pray for us.
St Paul, that we may awake and sin no more, *Pray for us.*
That we may not receive the grace of God in vain, *Pray for us.*
That we may walk in newness of life, *Pray for us.*
That we may work out our salvation with fear and trembling,
   Pray for us.
That we may put on the armour of God, *Pray for us.*
That we may stand against the deceits of the wicked one, *Pray for us.*
That we may stand fast to the last, *Pray for us.*
That we may press forward to the mark, *Pray for us.*
That we may win the crown, *Pray for us.*

Lamb of God, who takes away the sins of the world:
   Spare us, O Lord.
Lamb of God, who takes away the sins of the world:
   Graciously hear us, O Lord.
Lamb of God, who takes away the sins of the world:
   Have mercy on us.

Let us pray. O God, who has taught the whole world by the
preaching of blessed Paul the Apostle: grant that we, who
celebrate his memory, may by following his example be drawn
to you. Through our Lord Jesus Christ, *Amen.*

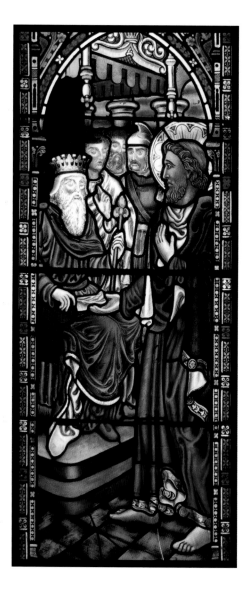

Peace with God through Christ

Therefore, since we are justified by faith, we have peace with God through our Lord Jesus Christ. Through him we have obtained access to this grace in which we stand, and we rejoice in our hope of sharing the glory of God. More than that, we rejoice in our sufferings, knowing that suffering produces endurance, and endurance produces character, and character produces hope, and hope does not disappoint us, because God's love has been poured into our hearts through the Holy Spirit which has been given to us. While we were still weak, at the right time Christ died for the ungodly. Why, one will hardly die for a righteous man – though perhaps for a good man one will dare even to die. But God shows his love for us in that while we were yet sinners Christ died for us. Since, therefore, we are now justified by his blood, much more shall we be saved by him from the wrath of God.

Romans 5: 1-9

Lord, on the cross you demonstrated your love for mankind, for by the sacrifice of your death you have paid the price of Adam's sin. We have faith in you O Lord; now you have begun your work in us, we pray that you may bring it to completion.

Amen

Athens was the centre of classical philosophy and culture. St Paul addressed the Stoic and Epicurean philosophers at the Areopagus, an important court in Athens. He argued that God was not material, and that the seeds of revelation were present even outside the Jewish tradition.

“ *Ever since the creation of the world his invisible nature, namely, his eternal power and deity, has been clearly perceived in the things that have been made.* ”

Romans 1: 20

The Speech at the Areopagus

'Men of Athens, I perceive that in every way you are very religious. For as I passed along, and observed the objects of your worship, I found also an altar with this inscription, "To an unknown god." What therefore you worship as unknown, this I proclaim to you. The God who made the world and everything in it, being Lord of heaven and earth, does not live in shrines made by man, nor is he served by human hands, as though he needed anything, since he himself gives to all men life and breath and everything. And he made from one every nation of men to live on all the face of the earth, having determined allotted periods and the boundaries of their habitation, that they should seek God, in the hope that they might feel after him and find him. Yet he is not far from each one of us, for "In him we live and move and have our being"; as even some of your poets have said, "For we are indeed his offspring." Being then God's offspring, we ought not to think that the Deity is like gold, or silver, or stone, a representation by the art and imagination of man.'

Acts 17: 22-29

God, your grace is unconfined, and through your Apostle Paul you made it known that your people are called from all nations. You called us even before we knew you; grant that we may ever seek you, and that one day we may see you face to face.

Amen

SCS PAULUS

Sedet hic Scripfa...

One Body in Christ

For just as the body is one and has many members, and all the members of the body, though many, are one body, so it is with Christ. For by one Spirit we were all baptized into one body – Jews or Greeks, slaves or free – and all were made to drink of one Spirit. For the body does not consist of one member but of many. God arranged the organs in the body, each one of them, as he chose. If all were a single organ, where would the body be? As it is, there are many parts, yet one body. The eye cannot say to the hand, "I have no need of you," nor again the head to the feet, "I have no need of you." On the contrary, the parts of the body which seem to be weaker are indispensable, and those parts of the body which we think less honourable we invest with the greater honour, and our unpresentable parts are treated with greater modesty, which our more presentable parts do not require. But God has so composed the body, giving the greater honour to the inferior part, that there may be no discord in the body, but that the members may have the same care for one another. If one member suffers, all suffer together; if one member is honoured, all rejoice together.

1 Corinthians 12: 12-14, 18-26

O God, through your Church you are with us, even to the end of the age. In the Church, your mystical body, may we be united to you, and in you may we be united to our fellow man. Together, may your children be one in will and affection, as we lift up our hearts to you, our common Father.

Amen

In this Hope we were Saved

We know that the whole creation has been groaning in travail together until now; and not only the creation, but we ourselves, who have the first fruits of the Spirit, groan inwardly as we wait for adoption as sons, the redemption of our bodies. For in this hope we were saved. Now hope that is seen is not hope. For who hopes for what he sees? But if we hope for what we do not see, we wait for it with patience. Likewise the Spirit helps us in our weakness; for we do not know how to pray as we ought, but the Spirit himself intercedes for us with sighs too deep for words. And he who searches the hearts of men knows what is the mind of the Spirit, because the Spirit intercedes for the saints according to the will of God.

Romans 8: 22-27

O God, wherever we look we see only our own limitations, our lack of strength and our helplessness. May we always have hope in the salvation Christ offers, who knows all our needs and answers every prayer.

Amen

We Are More than Conquerors

Who shall separate us from the love of Christ? Shall tribulation, or distress, or persecution, or famine, or nakedness, or peril, or sword? As it is written, 'For thy sake we are being killed all the day long; we are regarded as sheep to be slaughtered.' No, in all these things we are more than conquerors through him who loved us. For I am sure that neither death, nor life, nor angels, nor principalities, nor things present, nor things to come, nor powers, nor height, nor depth, nor anything else in all creation, will be able to separate us from the love of God in Christ Jesus our Lord.

Romans 8: 35-39

Lord, you are closer to us than we are to ourselves. Because you conquered death by your resurrection, we shall fear no evil, nor any tribulation, when we unite ourselves to you in your love.

Amen

The Helmet of Salvation

But you are not in darkness, brethren. For you are all sons of light and sons of the day; we are not of the night or of darkness. So then let us not sleep, as others do, but let us keep awake and be sober. For those who sleep sleep at night, and those who get drunk are drunk at night. But, since we belong to the day, let us be sober, and put on the breastplate of faith and love, and for a helmet the hope of salvation. For God has not destined us for wrath, but to obtain salvation through our Lord Jesus Christ, who died for us so that whether we wake or sleep we might live with him. Therefore encourage one another and build one another up, just as you are doing.

1 Thessalonians 5: 4-11

Saint Paul, you suffered much to proclaim the Gospel to the world, and in all your sufferings you were fortified by the love of God. Like you, may we who are weak allow Christ to defend us, who by his death has assured us of final victory.

Amen

The Basilica of St Paul Outside the Walls in Rome, erected over the site of the Apostle's grave.

I Bow My Knees Before the Father

For this reason I bow my knees before the Father, from whom every family in heaven and on earth is named, that according to the riches of his glory he may grant you to be strengthened with might through his Spirit in the inner man, and that Christ may dwell in your hearts through faith; that you, being rooted and grounded in love, may have power to comprehend with all the saints what is the breadth and length and height and depth, and to know the love of Christ which surpasses knowledge, that you may be filled with all the fullness of God.

Ephesians 3: 14-19

Lord, in you there is nothing evil; when we turn to you we turn away from sin. Grant us through your Spirit the sevenfold gifts of grace, that they may flourish into their ninefold fruits, and that we may be thereby ever conformed to your image.

Amen

Inside the Basilica of St Paul Outside the Walls

You Must Bear Witness in Rome

*After three missionary journeys around the
Mediterranean, Paul was arrested in Jerusalem
for supposedly bringing a gentile, Trophimus,
into the Temple. As a Roman citizen, Paul was
entitled to demand a trial in Rome.*

But Paul said, 'I am standing before
Caesar's tribunal, where I ought to be
tried; to the Jews I have done no wrong,
as you know very well. If then I am a
wrongdoer, and have committed anything
for which I deserve to die, I do not seek
to escape death; but if there is nothing in
their charges against me, no one can give
me up to them. I appeal to Caesar.' Then
Festus, when he had conferred with his
council, answered, 'You have appealed to
Caesar; to Caesar you shall go.'

Acts 25: 10-12

Father give us your strength, that we may trust in
your word, whatever the circumstances of our
lives, and in whatever you have called us to do. Give
us the grace to persevere even to the end.

Amen

The ship in which St Paul was being brought to Rome foundered. The Apostle was washed up on what is now known as St Paul's Bay, on the north coast of Malta. He converted the local population, and is today a patron of the island.

Shipwreck

Now when it was day, they did not recognise the land, but they noticed a bay with a beach, on which they planned if possible to bring the ship ashore. The soldiers' plan was to kill the prisoners, lest any should swim away and escape; but the centurion, wishing to save Paul, kept them from carrying out their purpose. He ordered those who could swim to throw themselves overboard first and make for the land, and the rest on planks or on pieces of the ship. And so it was that all escaped to land. After we had escaped, we then learned that the island was called Malta. And the natives showed us unusual kindness, for they kindled a fire and welcomed us all, because it had begun to rain and was cold.

Acts 27: 39, 42 – 28: 2

Great convert and Apostle of the Gentiles, you became Christlike and knew only Christ Crucified. Though extremely learned, you relied completely on the Wisdom received from the Spirit and taught from the abundance of your heart. Instruct those who preach Christ to others in the modern world, that they may rely above all on the promptings of the Spirit.

Amen

St Paul was beheaded in Rome on the orders of the Emperor Nero. According to tradition, his severed head bounced three times along the ground, a fountain springing up in each place. The abbey of Tre Fontane is built on the site, and the springs still flow today. St Paul's body was buried nearby; his followers erected a memorial over the grave, which the Emperor Constantine replaced with St Paul's Basilica.

I Have Kept the Faith

For I am already on the point of being sacrificed; the time of my departure has come. I have fought the good fight, I have finished the race, I have kept the faith. Henceforth there is laid up for me the crown of righteousness, which the Lord, the righteous judge, will award to me on that Day, and not only to me but also to all who have loved his appearing.

2 Timothy 4: 6-8

O God, you granted St Paul the grace of becoming a martyr for the faith. We know that you always give us the strength to carry the load; we pray that, like your Apostle, we too may find courage to bear witness to the truth in the way you desire for us.

Amen

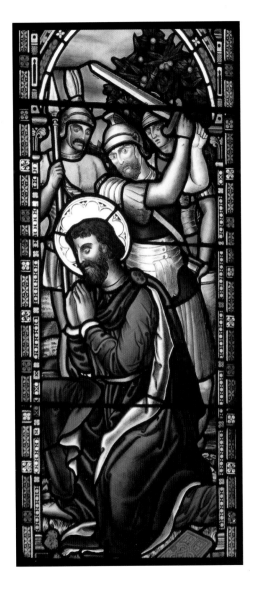

Martyrdom

The Acts of the Apostles, written by St Paul's companion, St Luke, breaks off with Paul in prison in Rome, and does not include the account of his martyrdom. His death is mentioned, however, by St Clement, the fourth Pope, in the letter he wrote to the Church in Corinth in about 96 A.D.

By reason of jealousy and strife Paul by his example pointed out the prize of patient endurance. After he had been seven times in bonds, had been driven into exile, had been stoned, had preached in the East and in the West, he won the noble renown which was the reward of his faith, having taught righteousness unto the whole world and having reached the farthest bounds of the West; and when he had borne his testimony before the rulers, so he departed from the world and went unto the holy place, having been found a notable pattern of patient endurance.

1 Clement 5: 5-6

Saint Paul, you joyfully endured all manner of persecutions, culminating in the shedding of the last drop of your blood for our Lord Jesus Christ. Help us to be inspired by your Epistles, so that after we have finished our course we may join you in praising Him in heaven for all eternity.

Amen

The exact site of St Paul's burial in Rome lies directly beneath the high altar in the Basilica of St Paul Outside the Walls.

Litany in Honour of St Paul

Charity of the Father, *Save us.*
Grace of our Lord Jesus Christ, *Vivify us.*
Communication of the Holy Spirit, *Sanctify us.*
Blessed Paul, *Pray for us.*
You who obtained the mercy of God, *Pray for us.*
You in whom the Son of God was revealed, *Pray for us.*
You who were a vessel of election for Christ, *Pray for us.*
You who were made preacher, apostle and doctor of the
   Gentiles in truth, *Pray for us.*

You whose apostolate was confirmed by marvels and
wonders, *Pray for us.*
You who were a most faithful minister of the Church,
Pray for us.
You who gave the nations the Gospel of Christ and your
very life, *Pray for us.*
You who carried the faithful in your heart and in your
chains, *Pray for us.*
You who were crucified with Christ, *Pray for us.*
You in whom Christ lived and spoke, *Pray for us.*
You whom nothing could separate from the love of
Christ, *Pray for us.*
You who underwent imprisonment and toil, *Pray for us.*
You who suffered wounds and dangers, *Pray for us.*
You who were taken into Heaven while still living on
earth, *Pray for us.*
You who glorified your ministry, *Pray for us.*
You who awaited the crown after completing your
mission, *Pray for us.*
Lamb of God, who converted the persecutor Paul, *Spare us.*
Lamb of God, who crowned the apostle Paul,
Graciously hear us.
Lamb of God, who glorified the martyr Paul,
Have mercy on us.
You are a vessel of election, St Paul the Apostle.
Preacher of truth throughout the world.

Let us pray. O God, you have instructed many nations
through the preaching of the blessed apostle, Paul.
May the power of his intercession with you help us to
venerate his memory this day, *Amen.*

O St Paul, chosen vessel of the Lord, who carried the name of Jesus to kings and heathens, who suffered so much for Christ, and was never allured from the love of Him: like a brave soldier of Christ, you fought a good battle, a zealous teacher, you preached far and wide the true faith, and the just and merciful God has, therefore, rewarded you with the crown of justice: pray to God for me, that I may become an instrument of honour, adorned with the Christian virtues, with which you are already decorated. Through Jesus Christ our Lord,

Amen